# 2000 Memories

## Jason and the Memory Box

Written by  Shelley Fiset

Illustrated by Aimée Chatelaine

This book is dedicated to all the men and women who served our country in Canada and overseas, and to the families who stayed behind.

Your sacrifice will never be forgotten.

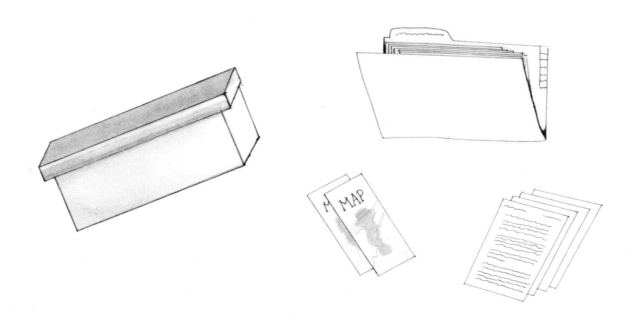

Jason was very excited. Today was the day he was going to visit his Grandma in Ottawa.

Grandma had called him to invite him for a visit. She told him she had a very special gift to give him. Something that belonged to his Grandfather.

Jason didn't remember his Grandfather. He died when Jason was little, but his mother always talked about him. He was very curious to see what Grandma's gift was.

Grandma met Jason at the airport.

"Welcome to Ottawa" Grandma told him giving him a great big hug.

It had been a long time since Jason had seen her, and he missed her very much.  Jason gave her a big hug back.

"I'm so glad you could make it Jason" Grandma said.

"I have something very special planned for you tomorrow.  And I have something very special to give to you today."

After they had arrived at Grandma's and rested for a bit, Grandma asked Jason to come into the living room. There on the floor beside the couch was a big wooden box that looked like a trunk.

Grandma called Jason over to sit beside her on the couch.

"This is my gift to you Jason," said Grandma, "this is a memory box. Because the year 2,000 is a very special year, I've decided to collect 2,000 memories of your Grandpa and what he did for Canada during the Second World War."

"We can go through the memory box together and count up all the memories. Some of them you will understand right away, but some of them you won't really understand until you are much older," she added.

Jason was very curious about what sorts of things could be in the box.

Grandma opened the lid.

"Before we begin," Grandma said, "you can use that notepad and pencil on the table to add up everything in the box to make sure it all adds up to 2,000."

Jason quickly took the pencil and notepad off the table.

Jason reached into the box and the first thing he pulled out was a little black book.

His Grandmother told him that it was a diary that belonged to his Grandfather.  She said his Grandpa tried to write something in the diary almost every day while he was away at war.  Grandpa was away for more than 4 years, she told him - so Jason knew that meant he must have made a lot of entries!

"1,234 to be exact," said Grandma.

Jason wrote down 1,234 in his notebook.

Jason reached in again and pulled out a square tin container about the size of a shoebox.

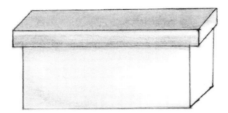

Inside the tin container were dozens and dozens of photos.

"There are **97** pictures in the tin," said Grandma. "I've tried to label the back of each one with a place and date".

Jason picked up one picture of two young men, arm-in-arm, smiling at the camera. When he flipped the picture over, it said "Joseph and Larry on their way to enlist - June 3, 1941."

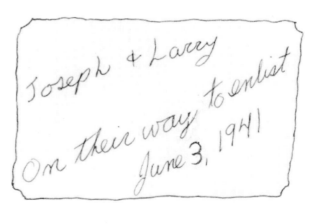

"Larry was your Grandpa's younger brother - he would be your Great-Uncle," Grandma told him. Jason thought Larry looked about the same age as his babysitter Tim.

Next came **8** medals.

"Some of these medals are your Grandpa's," said Grandma, "and some of them belonged to your Uncle Larry. Your Mom told me she'll take you to the library sometime soon to look up what each medal means on the internet," she added.

1,331
+ 8
1,339

Then came a package of letters and postcards tied up in a bright red ribbon.

"These are the letters your Grandpa and I wrote to each other when he was away," said Grandma.

"There are 114 in total.  I kept every one your Grandfather ever wrote to me - all 113 of them," she said.

"Grandpa was only able to keep 1 of the letters I wrote to him. He kept it in his pocket at all times.  It was the letter that I replied that I would marry him," she said with a smile.  "That's it on the very top."

1,339
+   114
1,453

"Here are your Uncle Larry's memories," said Grandma as Jason began to pull out several different items that were bound together.

One $(1)$ of the items was a beautiful colour page of the Book of Remembrance.

"Your Uncle's name is in a Book of Remembrance in the Peace Tower here in Ottawa," Grandma told him. "His name was put in that book along with all the other young men and women who never made it back home. On a special day, once a year, a member of the House of Commons Service Staff turns the page of the Book and your Uncle's name appears on top for everyone to see for that day. This is a copy of the page where his name appears," she said.

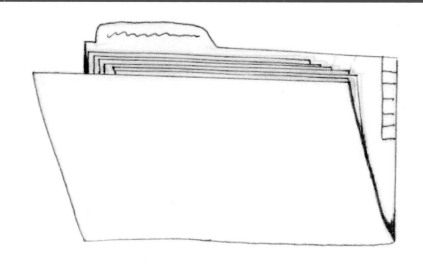

Grandma also showed Jason **6** pages of records she had received from the National Archives of Canada.

"This is from the place where all the records of anyone who served in the Canadian Armed Forces are stored," she told him.

She also had **2** maps and **4** pages of information from a place called the Commonwealth War Graves Commission.

"Grandpa's records from the National Archives are also here," said Grandma.

There was a total of 26 pages of information about him.

1,466
+   26
1,492

Next, Jason pulled out 2 things - 1 funny looking hat and 1 pair of white gloves.

"These were part of your Grandfather's "dress up" uniform he would wear when he had to attend special occasions," Grandma told him.

"One of the last special occasions he attended was at a pilgrimage he went on a few years ago. Veterans Affairs Canada invited your Grandpa and a group of other veterans to return to the United Kingdom to commemorate the anniversary of The Battle of the Atlantic." she said. "When you are a little older, you can read some of the booklets I've received from Veterans Affairs that tell all about the war. I've put them in the box with Grandpa's records."

$$1,492 \atop + \phantom{0}2 \over 1,494$$

"And here are **4** buttons he saved from his jacket," she added.

"And **1** ID card he had to carry at all times."

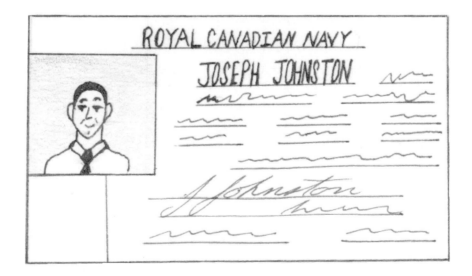

Jason then pulled out.....

**1** prayer book

**2** ration books

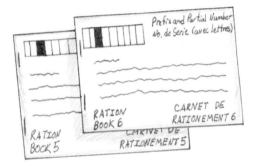

**1** Book of
Victory Stamps

And **2** cans of something called C-Rations.
One was peanut butter and the other was
cheese spread.

Jason looked at the 55 year old peanut
butter and wondered what it would taste like.

Then came.......

**1** pay book

And finally **2** sweetheart handkerchiefs.

"A soldier would buy their sweetheart a handkerchief and send it to her. This is one your Grandpa bought for me," she said.

"This one he bought for his other sweetheart - his mother," she added with a little smile.

Finally, the last thing Jason pulled out of the memory box was a little yellow book.

"That's my diary," said Grandma. "I didn't start it until the last year or so before the war ended, so I don't have as many entries in it as your Grandpa's."

"But I did manage to make 491 entries in all," she told him.

"You'll be able to read all about what it was like for those of us who stayed behind, on the homefront,"Grandma said. "Many people, including women, played a very important role in the war effort right here in Canada - from recycling, to rationing, to working in factories," she added.

1,508
+ 491
1,999

Jason looked at the notepad where he had added up all the items he had pulled out of the memory box.

The total was at **1,999**.

He reached into the box to pull out the final item that would give him a grand total of 2,000 memories, but to his surprise, the box was now empty.

"Did I miss one Grandma?" Asked Jason in confusion. I only counted 1,999 memories. "Where's the last memory?" he asked her.

Grandma just smiled and told Jason that he didn't miss one, that there was only 1,999 memories in the box.

"The last item for the box isn't ready yet," she told him. "It will be ready by tomorrow. Rest now, because we have a very big day ahead," she added.

Jason closed his eyes and went to sleep thinking about what the final item could possibly be.

The next day, Grandma got Jason out of bed early.

"We have a very special day today," she said. "Today we are going to a ceremony at the local cenotaph."

WE WILL
REMEMBER THEM

1914
1918

1939
1945

KOREA

1950
1953

IN FLANDERS FIELDS...

BRANCH
887
ROYAL CANADIAN LEGION

Grandma told Jason that a cenotaph was a special monument that was erected in almost every town in Canada. It was done to remind everyone about all the men and women who went to war and died.

On the 11th hour of the 11th day of the 11th month, a special ceremony is held at all the cenotaphs across the country to honour those men and women.

| NOVEMBER 1999 NOVEMBRE | | | | | | |
|---|---|---|---|---|---|---|
| | 1 | 2 | 3 | 4 | 5 | 6 |
| 7 | 8 | 9 | 10 | 11 | 12 | 13 |
| 14 | 15 | 16 | 17 | 18 | 19 | 20 |
| 21 | 22 | 23 | 24 | 25 | 26 | 27 |
| 28 | 29 | 30 | | | | |

"Today is November 11th - Remembrance Day," Grandma told him. "We are going to attend the ceremony at the cenotaph so we can remember together."

Just before they left, Grandma pinned a bright red poppy to Jason's coat.

"The poppy is our symbol for remembering," she told him. "We wear it over our hearts to show that we have not forgotten the sacrifices that were made for our freedom."

"When we come back from the cenotaph," Grandma told Jason, "you can place this poppy in your memory box to remind you of what we did today to remember your Grandpa and your Uncle Larry."

"This **1** poppy will be the last item for your memory box to make the grand total of **2,000** memories," she said.

"It is my hope that this memory box will encourage you to remember not only on Remembrance Day, but throughout the year as well," she added.

1,999
+   1
2,000

At the cenotaph, the man at the front talked about how it was important that we don't forget all of the people who had to go to war and that they did it to keep us free.  He asked everyone to bow their heads and take 2 minutes of silence to remember them. And to thank them.

Jason bowed his head.

He thought about the memory box that his Grandma had made for him.

He thought about his Uncle Larry who wasn't much older than Tim who babysat him sometimes.

And as the silence continued, Jason thought about his Grandpa...................

# Definitions

**C-Rations:** Soldiers sometimes carried either a 24 or 48 hour pack of emergency rations. A typical C-Ration pack could contain such items as 5 graham crackers, a tin of peanut butter, a tin of cheese spread, compressed liver, a bit of chocolate and compressed tea (which was milk, sugar & tea compressed down into the size of a bouillon cube)

**Stamp Books:** Victory Stamps, purchased for as little as a quarter, could be glued into a savings booklet. When filled, the booklet became a $4 War Savings Certificate, which could be redeemed with the Canadian Government after 7 years for $5. Businesses would often offer Victory Stamps as change.

**Ration Books:** The Wartime Prices & Trade Board introduced coupon rationing in 1942. Each family received a booklet of coupons every few months. Examples of items that were rationed included; coffee, tea, sugar, butter.

**Sweetheart Handkerchiefs:** A soldier would often buy their "sweetheart" a handkerchief from the country they were stationed in or passing through. They would send it back home with their letters. Ladies also bought handkerchiefs to wave at the marching troops.

**Pay Books:** Everyone was required to carry their pay book in order to receive their pay. It was also commonly used for identification purposes.

**Commonwealth War Graves Commission:** Established by Royal Charter shortly after the end of the First World War, the Commission's duties are to mark and maintain the graves of the members of the forces of the Commonwealth who were killed during the two World Wars. They also are responsible to build memorials to those who have no known grave and to keep records and registers.

**Books of Remembrance:** The 6 Books of Remembrance contain the names of Canadians who fought in wars and died either during or after them. They are kept in the Memorial Chamber located in the Peace Tower on Parliament Hill. All together, the 6 books contain a total of 114,710 names.

**Remembrance Day:** Remembrance Day commemorates Canadians who died in the First and Second World Wars and the Korean War. It is held every November 11. Originally called Armistice Day, it commemorated the end of the First World War on Monday, November 11, 1918 at 11:00 a.m. - the 11th hour of the 11th day of the 11th month. A bill was passed in 1931 and the first official Remembrance Day was conducted on November 11, 1931.

**Poppy:** The poppy is the symbol for Remembrance Day. Replica poppies are sold by the Royal Canadian Legion to raise money for needy veterans.

**2 minutes of silence/The Wave of Silence:** On the 11th Hour, of the 11th day, of the 11th month! The Royal Canadian Legion is calling on all Canadians - wherever they may be - to remember the service and sacrifice of Canadians in wartime by observing two minutes of silence at 11:00 a.m. on November 11 - Remembrance Day! Why not organize two minutes of silence in your community?